Simple Lace and

Beaded Jewelry Patterns

(For Ages 7 to 70)

by

Mary Ellen Harte

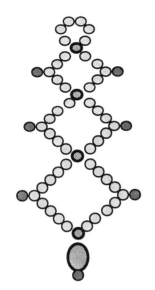

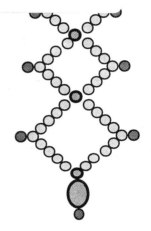

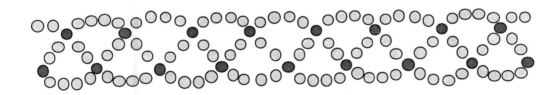

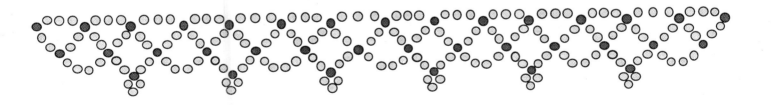

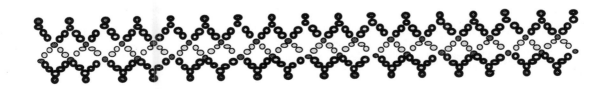

Eagle's View Publishing Company
A WestWind, Inc. Company
6756 North Fork Road
Liberty, UT 84310

Library of Congress Number: 96-85695
ISBN 0-943604-55-9

15 14 13 12 11 10 9 8 7 6 5 4 3 2

TABLE OF CONTENTS

Introduction, Materials and Methods   5-7
Types of Beads   7
Simple Chain Variations   8
Ball and Loop Clasp   9
Lace Loop Chain I & II   10-11
Lace Loop Necklace with Diamonds   12
Lace Diamond Pattern   13
Multi-Diamond Pattern   14
Medallion Pattern   15
Pretzel Loop Pattern   16
Flower Chain I & II   17-18
Hour Glass Loop Pattern   19
Pagoda Earrings   20
Dangling Diamond Earrings   21
Spider Web Earrings   22
Chain Link Necklace   23
Hula Hoop Necklace   24
Pennant Choker Necklace   25
Julia's Necklace   26
Empress Choker Necklace   27
Hanging Bead Necklace   28
Julia's Loopy Necklace   29
Valentine Necklace *   30

* OK, not so simple, but doable once you get this far . . .

ILLUSTRATIONS
Front Cover - Pages 21 and 30
Back Cover - Page 25

DEDICATION

To my beloved helper and inspiration,
my daughter, Julia,
and
To my beloved and supportive husband, John.

ABOUT THE AUTHOR

Mary Ellen ("Mel") Harte is a marine biologist, mother and craftsperson whose passion for pattern overflows into her other passions, beadwork and folkdancing. An avid collector of ethnic textiles and crafts, she attempted to recreate a native American beaded flower ring and pass the skill to her daughter.

Deciphering existing bead patterns and creating her own, she taught other children as well. This book evolved from that work. She migrates between Berkeley, CA and the Colorado Rockies.

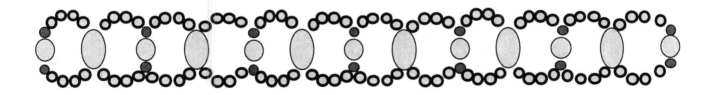

Introduction

Lace beadwork extends across many cultures. The Guaymi women of Costa Rica create large, elaborate, brightly colored diamond lace necklaces; Romanian and Hungarian women produce beautiful, delicate, and sometimes complex geometric lace necklaces. Zulus and other Africans create brightly colored beadwork to adorn not only themselves but gourd drums. In Papua New Guinea I collected brightly colored loop lace and diamond lace bracelets, as well as flower chain necklaces years ago; more recently these same flower or daisy chains have come into fashion in the U. S. as eyeglass chains. Native Americans also practice the art. Unlike woven beadwork, no loom is involved; the lacy patterns are created through the interconnection of repeating patterns, some of which can get fairly involved. The good news, though, is that you can make beautiful examples with relatively simple patterns.

This book illustrates several relatively simple beading patterns to create lacy beaded rings, bracelets (or napkin holders), necklaces and earrings, many of which, especially the bracelets, I have taught to children as young as seven years.

Materials

Most materials discussed here are available through bead shops or mail order businesses. Use glass or "Indian" **seed beads**. These vary in size; if you decide to use very small ones, you might have to change your thread and needle size accordingly. Seed beads are usually round, but can be polygonal ("hex cut" or "two cut"), multifaceted ("3 cut" or "charlottes") or cylindrical (delicas), the latter usually used for bead weaving and looms. Beads can be opaque, translucent or clear, and come in a variety of finishes (e. g., iridescent, opalescent, silver lined, galvanized, matte, supra-luster, metallic). Many of the metallic finishes (and some inner linings) wear or wash off easily, so beware. Often, you can substitute bugle beads (slender cylindrical glass beads varying from 5-30 mm in length) for straight lengths of seed beads to achieve a different effect. Use the same size seed bead throughout your chosen project, unless otherwise noted. I use **size 10/° or 11/° seed beads. Buy strands (hanks) of beads;** this allows you to thread several at a time. Get **larger (at least 6mm) glass beads** as needed.

Unless noted otherwise in the patterns, I use **4 lb test monofilament** (a size of nylon fishing line available at sport/fishing stores) for most bracelets and necklaces. Monofilament doesn't tangle as much as beading thread, and stretches, as when stretching a bracelet over your wrist, a ring around your finger, or a choker around your neck. Although the developing piece might bunch somewhat initially, the finished piece stretches flat with wear. For delicate pieces, such as earrings, single or simple chain necklaces, and necklaces involving relatively few interconnections (e. g., Hanging Bead Necklace, Julia's Loopy Necklace) however, use **beading thread (Nymo brand, Size A or O)**, not fishing line, to avoid permanent kinks developing either during construction or storage afterwards. Beading thread holds both beads and knots in position (no slippage). Use a color that blends best with the beads. Ultimately you should decide which thread to use for each piece yourself, but be prepared to modify the patterns here slightly if you decide to use other than the suggested thread for each piece.

Although long slender **beading needles** are popular for threading beads, they require very thin thread and can be difficult to thread without needle threaders. Instead, I use **Sharp, size 12 Needles.** Needle sizes are not standardized and vary by brand. For a work surface, use a **slightly rough cloth** (a cotton dish towel; a jeweler's **velvet pad** or **velvet covered board** is ideal) to prevent beads from rolling, and **narrow masking tape** for flagging the ends of working threads. Snip excess thread with **fine, sharp scissors.** Finished necklaces and earrings should be attached to **jump rings** and **clasps** or **earring findings** with **long nosed pliers**. I prefer spring clasps over barrel clasps, which can unscrew while in use.

If you plan to do several bead projects, you might want to create a **bead threading board**: Take a foot long smooth plank of wood and saw five or six shallow, narrow, parallel grooves or rills along its length, spaced a half inch apart (use a table saw). Buy hanks of threaded beads, and separate out single threads of desired colors and lay them in the rills. Place your index finger lightly over each thread, gently pull the thread out from the desired length of beads, and gently roll away your finger, being careful to push back any sticking beads. With the beads lined up, they can now be threaded easily. A **metal ruler with a central rill** is also good.

Methods

Before beginning work on a piece, think about your color combinations, and try to **layout your design.** Map out your color design by placing beads on the diagrams provided to remind you how many of what color to thread before joining them through the next connecting bead (**referred to throughout this book as a connector bead, and usually indicated as a dark bead**). If you find it initially confusing and difficult to focus on small beads, **practice with large beads & string** before using seed beads & thread. If you use different size large beads (as in the Medallion pattern), take into account how many of the seed beads you will need, if any, to compensate so that the repeating patterns are the same size. Snip off one foot of nylon thread and do a short sequence to **test your design**, if necessary. While I have tested all the designs in this book, I have not tested all the possible designs indicated in the *variation* section of each pattern. (There are literally hundreds!)

To start, **cut off 2-3 feet of thread**, and fold a piece of **masking tape** on itself to form a small flag on the thread about 3 inches from the end. Leave about 3 inches of thread when you end the piece as well. The tape will keep beads from falling off and once removed the remaining adhesive will help in binding the knots. The 3 inch ends will allow you to tie them together or to a jump ring (as in the Lace Loop Necklace with Diamonds), and then hide the ends by threading back through existing beadwork.

Lay out strands of the beads to be used, each strand taped at one end. When threading small groups of the same colored bead, use your thumb and forefinger to **pull off and hold a line of beads** that you can then skewer and thread with the needle. Once you start a piece, **keep the beadwork taut**, so that the nylon thread does not show between beads. This can be accomplished if you hold the last segment of beadwork between your thumb and forefinger while you attach the newest segment. Do not work more than a few inches off the work surface. **When you run out of thread**, cut off a new length, knot it to a two inch length of the end thread (I use three square knots), thread one inch of the ends back through existing beadwork to hide them (snipping off excess), and continue with the new thread. Repeat the bead pattern as many times as necessary to create the length of the piece suited for your purposes.

All the patterns are repeating, but you can **vary the designs** through different pattern and color combinations and modifications. For example, in the flower chain pattern, the first pattern forms a flower by placing six beads of the same color around a middle bead of a different color — but the second, identical pattern forms leaves by making the top, bottom and middle of the flower the same color (see the diagram). You can vary the patterns for slightly different effects. For example, you can vary the loop lace pattern by changing the number of (1) outside beads, (2) the connector beads, and/or (3) the inside beads occurring between the connector beads. You can also **mix patterns** — separating flower patterns with single threads, for example. You'll be surprised at the number of different designs you can personally create by mixing and varying patterns and colors. **Start with the simpler designs first !**

In order **to end a piece** by joining the beginning to the end part, put both ends near each other, and visualize what new beads it will take to create one more pattern to connect the opposing end patterns. Placing the ends next to a pattern diagram and comparing the diagram with the beadwork helps. The joining pattern will have beads from the ending and beginning pattern, and probably a few extras. A diagram helps you to do this for the flower chain pattern, but it is a good exercise to figure out joining patterns for the rest of the patterns given here yourself. Once you **attach the ends together or to jump rings, hide end threads** by working one inch of each thread back through the beadwork. **Snip** off any remaining thread.

Good Luck, and Happy Beading !!

TYPES OF SEED BEADS

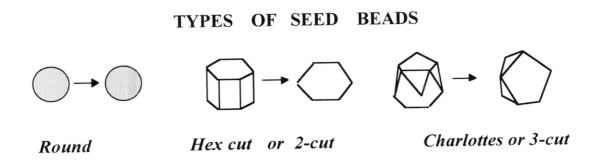

Round   Hex cut or 2-cut   Charlottes or 3-cut

SIMPLE CHAIN VARIATIONS

Use beading thread. String beads along one thread to create a first thread, then go through the first thread with a second thread, adding beads on at CONNECTOR beads, i. e., beads that connect more than one thread of beads, to create simple necklaces and bracelets. *Variations*: Substitute seed beads for bugle beads, vary the space between patterns.

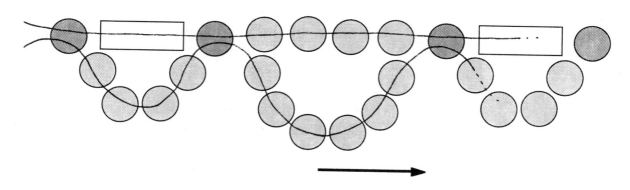

HALF MOON PATTERNS

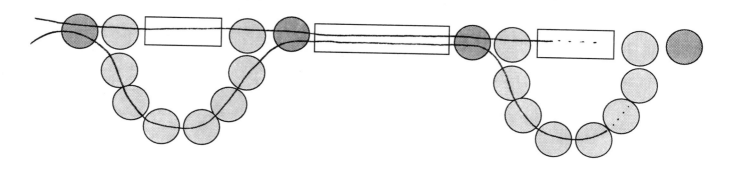

FLOWERING VINE PATTERN

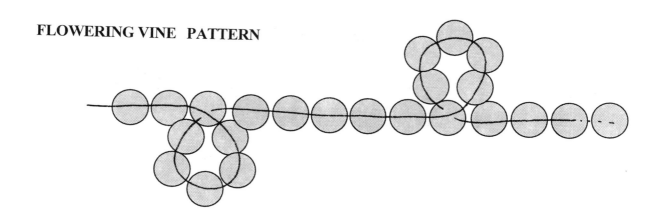

BALL & LOOP CLASP

If you don't want a continuous piece, you can make a beaded clasp rather than attach a jewelry clasp. Use a large (5mm or more in diameter) round plastic bead as the "ball." You can create the clasp as part of the entire piece or add it on later by threading the knotted clasp thread through existing beadwork first to anchor it.

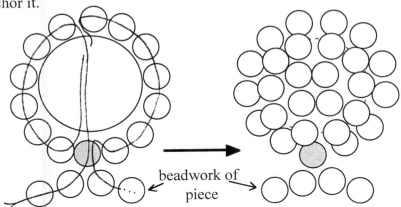

beadwork of piece

Thread through a bottom connector bead (colored), then through the big bead. Thread on enough seed beads to cover the length of the thread from the top to the bottom of the outside of the big bead. Bring the thread down to the bottom of the big bead (next to the connector bead) and rethread through the big bead again, adding on another row of seed beads. Keep repeating this until the outside of the big bead is covered with rows of seed beads. When you're adding your last row, make sure the seed bead at the top of the big bead for that row covers any "bald spot" there. Now thread through the connector bead, and continue the beadwork piece, or rethread through an inch of existing beadwork, knot it, rethread through another inch of beadwork, and trim the end. The ball fits into a loop attached in the same way to the other end of the piece. Check the fitness of the loop to the ball before ending the loop, adding beads as necessary! Loop:

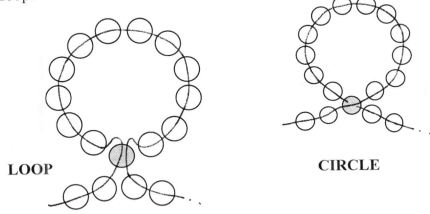

LOOP

CIRCLE

Note the difference between LOOPS and CIRCLES of beads, often a point of confusion for children: in loops, the thread enters the connector bead at the same opening from which it originates, as above; in circles, the thread originates from one opening and connects through the other opening (as in FLOWERING VINE on Pages 11 and 12).

LACE LOOP CHAIN I

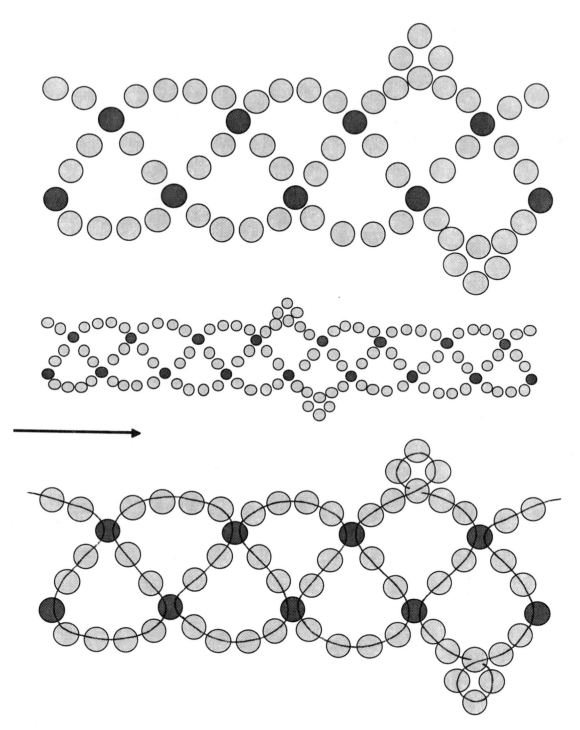

You can make bracelets or long chain necklaces with this pattern. Loops of beads are connected by looping the thread twice through a connector (dark) bead. Begin and end at a connector. About 40-50 loops creates a bracelet, or you can vary a section of 3-4 lace loops with a single string of beads to create simple necklaces. *Variations:* Replace inside beads with short bugle beads, or add little circles of three beads on the outer loops for added effect. The next page offers an example of other variations.

LACE LOOP CHAIN II

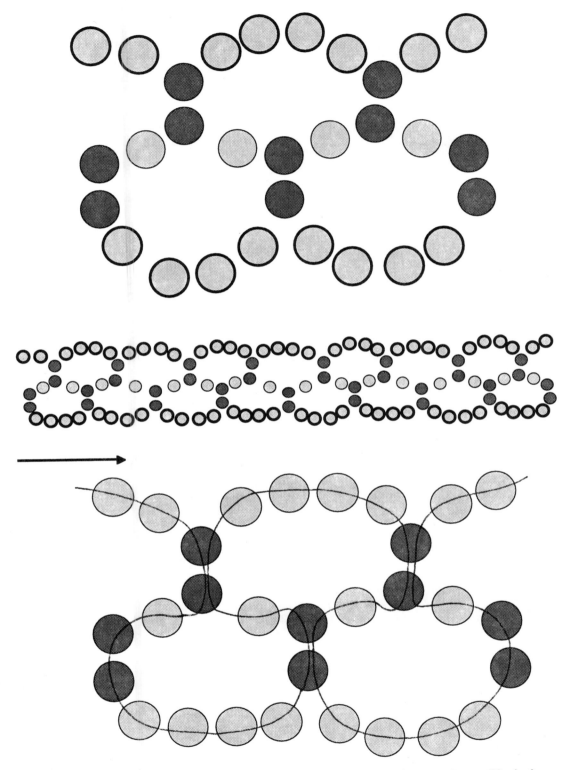

This is a variation of **LACE LOOP CHAIN I**; refer to it for basic instructions. ***Variations***: vary the number of connector (dark) or light beads for different effects. Write down and follow one pattern for your piece. Hint: the more outside beads (dark rimmed light ones, top), the loopier the bracelet gets.

LACE LOOP NECKLACE WITH DIAMONDS

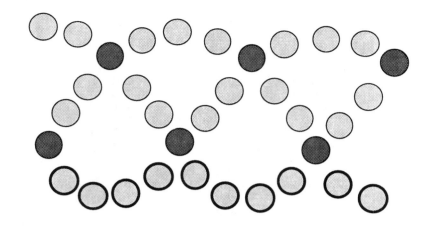

This pattern is just like **LACE LOOP CHAIN I**, but there are only three beads on the top outside part, while the bottom outside part has four (dark rimmed light beads). This causes the resulting chain to arch slightly, creating a natural curve, perfect for a short necklace. A Romanian necklace starts with an upper loop and places, after every 17 loops, hanging trios of beads to create the diamonds shown here:

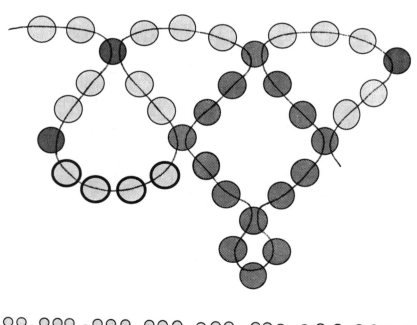

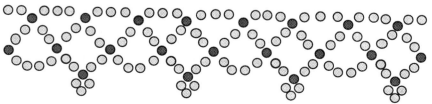

LACE DIAMOND PATTERN

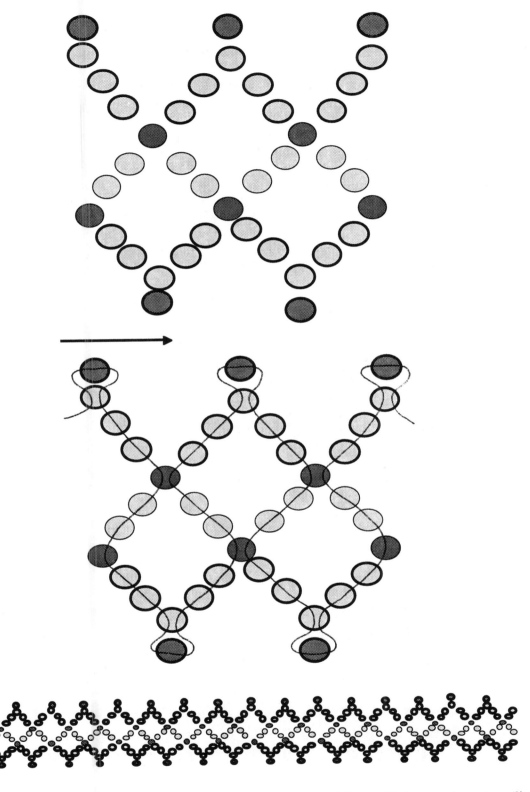

As in the **LACE LOOP CHAINS,** you can vary the number of inner (light ones), outer (light dark rimmed), and connector beads (dark ones) for different effects.

MULTI-DIAMOND PATTERN

Taken from a Zulu piece with a beaded ball and clasp, this design makes a wider bracelet, allowing you to create different colored designs of diamonds within the beadwork. One design is shown here, but try creating your own. Note that the edge diamonds are "rounded off" on the edges as in Hour Glass Loop Pattern. When you reach your desired length, wend the thread back through existing beadwork to the beginning and knot with the beginning thread. Create a beaded ball and clasp separately and attach.

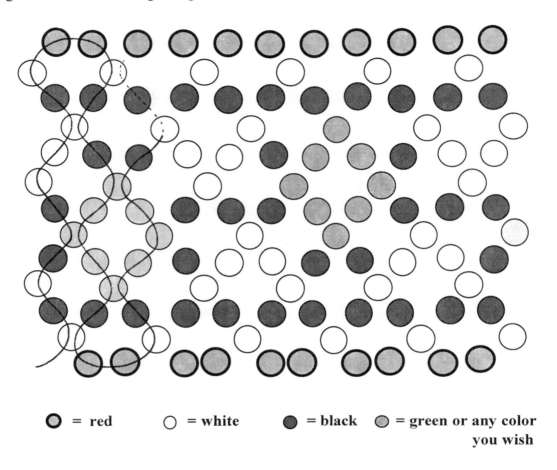

○ = red   ○ = white   ● = black   ◐ = green or any color
                                                              you wish

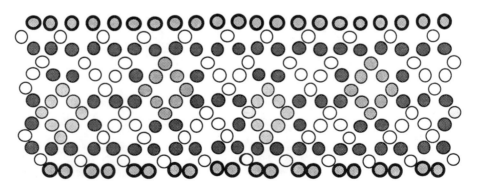

MEDALLION PATTERN

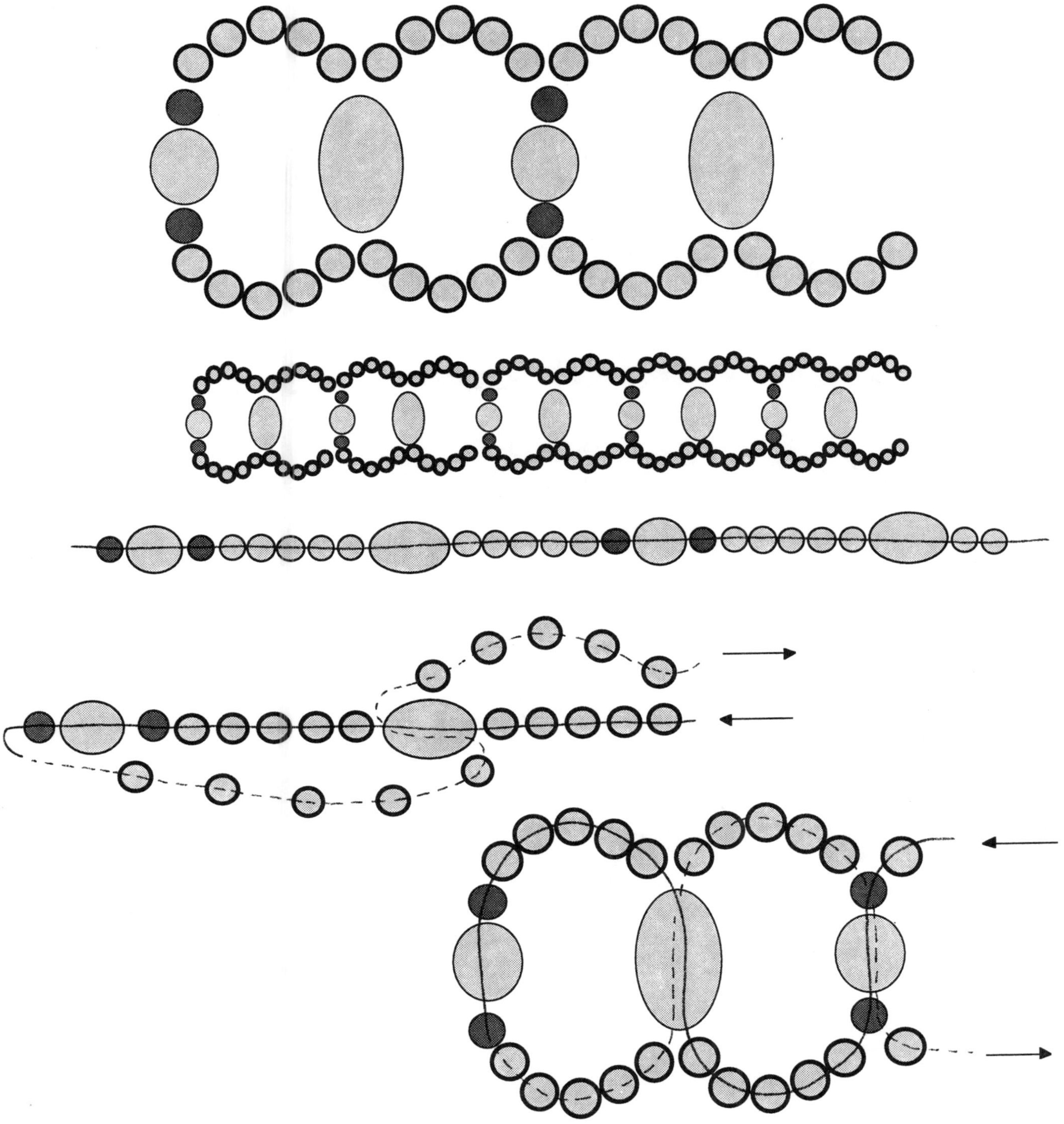

Thread all the medallion beads or sequences, spaced by five seed beads, in a complete string as shown above, ending in five seed beads; go back and loop through the next to last medallion, then pull taut to form the loop with two central medallions. Add another seed bead sequence, loop through the next medallion, pull taut, and continue. End by looping through the first medallion, add five outside beads and loop through the last medallion, tying a knot with the beginning thread. Vary by changing the number of seed beads, connector beads and medallions. An eight inch bracelet uses 22 medallions.

PRETZEL LOOP PATTERN

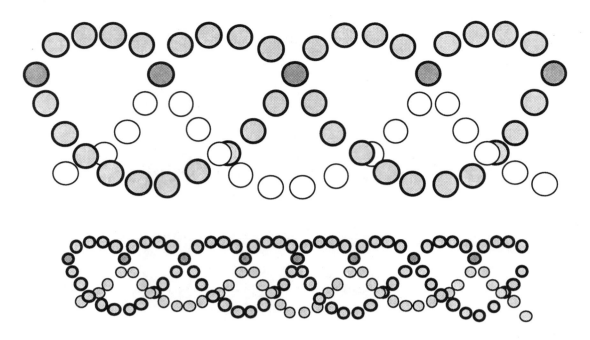

This bracelet has overlapping loops that give it a bulkier look. These lower, larger loops add greater elasticity, so this can also be used for a ropy necklace. Start with a connector bead; add 20 more beads (four tops, one connector, 10 bottoms, one connector, four tops), and loop through the first connector bead. After this start, add more sequences by adding 15 beads (four tops, one connector, 10 bottoms) at a time, then looping through the next available attached connector bead. Remember when attaching the ends to visualize the beads needed to complete the connecting pattern. *Variations*: Vary the number of connector beads, beads in the upper loops, and overlapping loops.

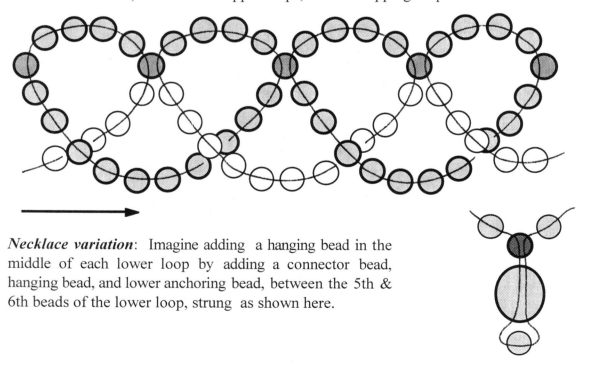

Necklace variation: Imagine adding a hanging bead in the middle of each lower loop by adding a connector bead, hanging bead, and lower anchoring bead, between the 5th & 6th beads of the lower loop, strung as shown here.

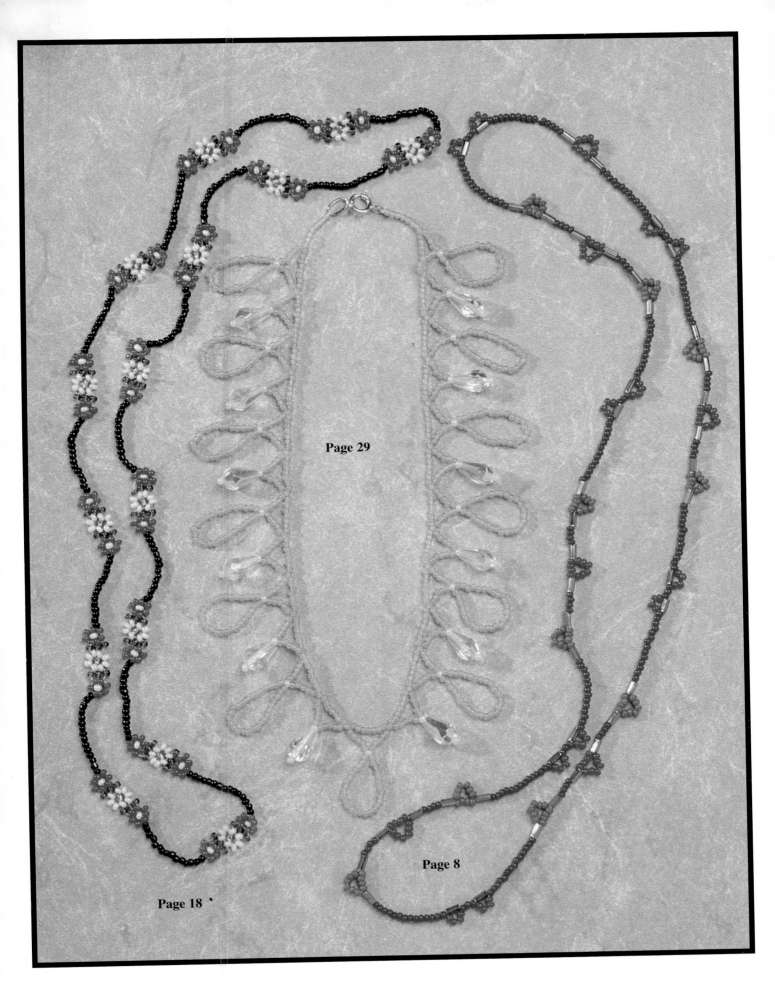

Page 29

Page 8

Page 18

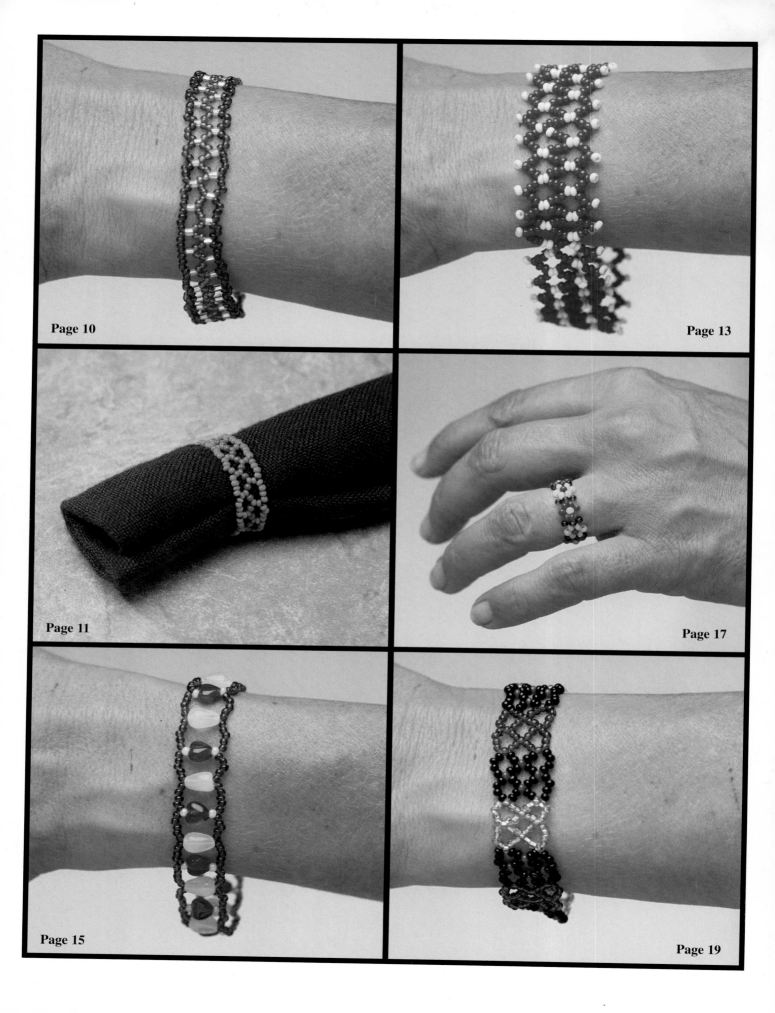

Page 10

Page 13

Page 11

Page 17

Page 15

Page 19

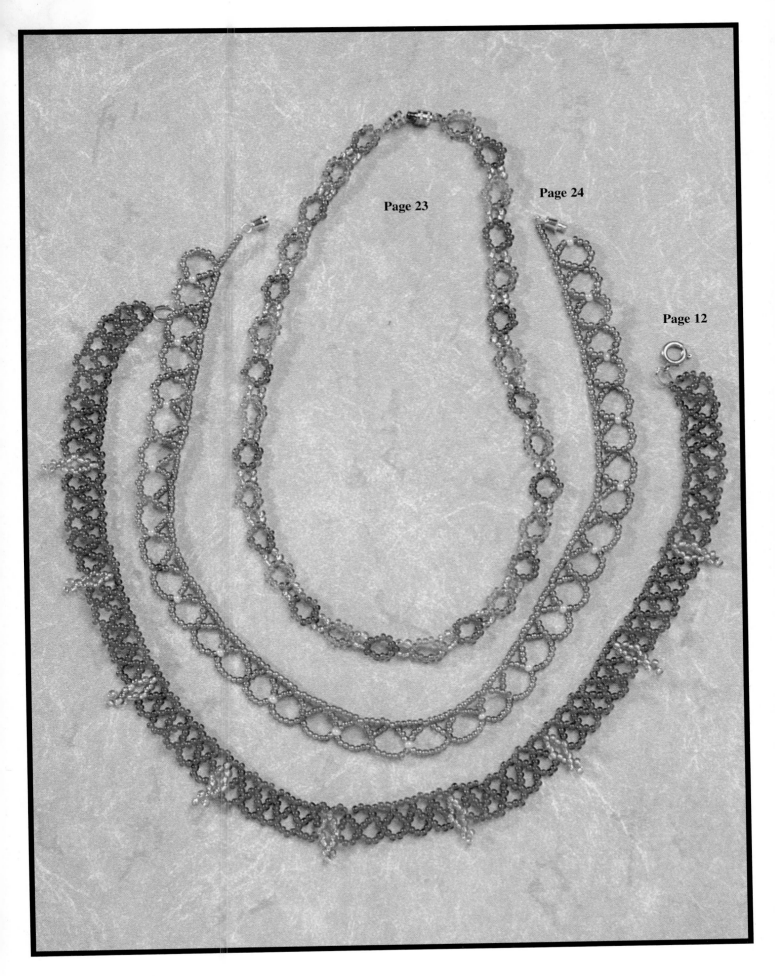

Page 23

Page 24

Page 12

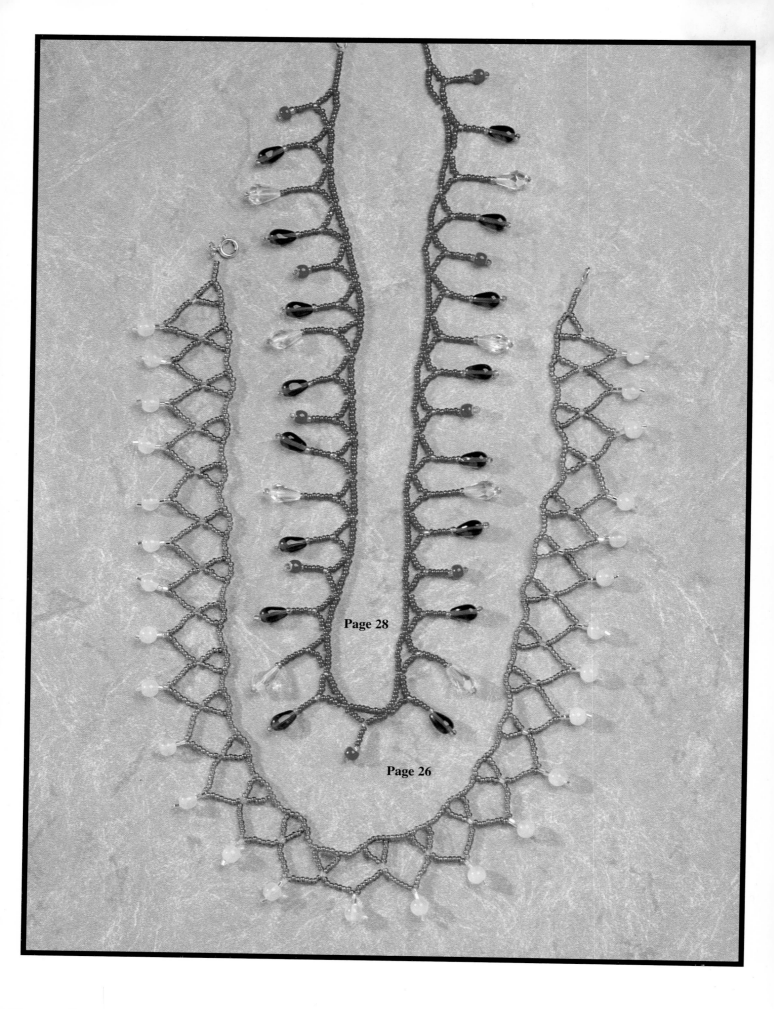

Page 28

Page 26

FLOWER CHAIN I

This pattern can be used to create rings or delicate necklaces or bracelets. In the first pattern six beads circle a central bead, but subsequently, only five beads -- a center and four circling beads (dark rimmed) -- are added. Two different threading patterns (A & B, below) create the same effect. A ring requires 16 patterns or more, depending on size.

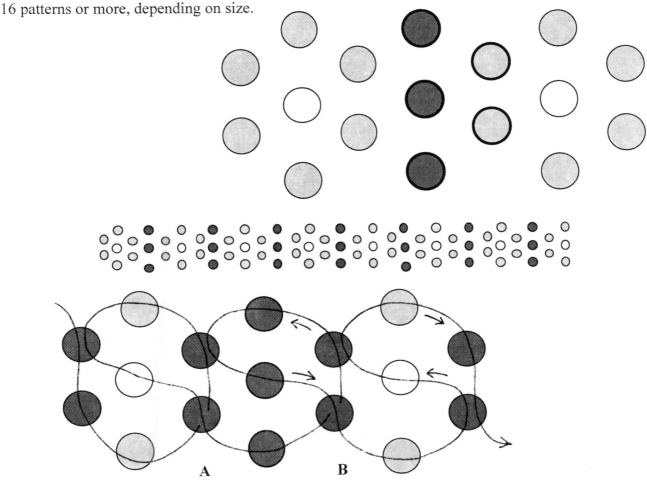

A   B

To join the ends, you add three beads (dark rimmed), joining them to the first beads (those with the dashed starting thread). Send the starting thread back through the last bead to join the end thread and knot them.

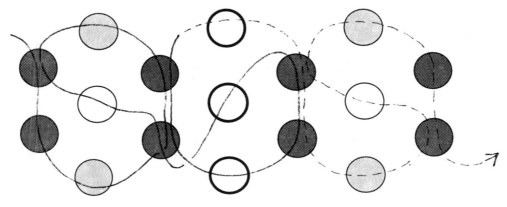

FLOWER CHAIN II

This chain can be used to make heavier bracelets and necklaces.

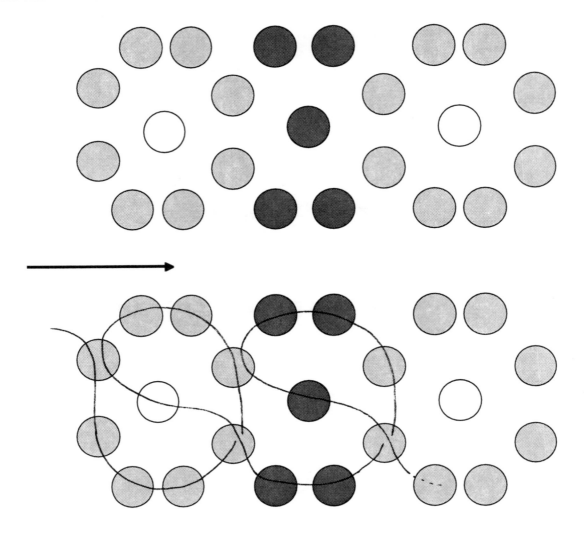

Variations: Intersperse one or more flower patterns between one inch or more thread lengths of seed and/or bugle beads to create simple necklaces, using beading thread. I made one of a trio of flowers interspersed with leaves (thus five flower patterns total - 7, 5, 9, 5, 7 bead petal patterns, respectively; the central larger one - 9 bead petals - had a larger bead for its center), separated by one inch lengths of black beads.

HOUR GLASS LOOP PATTERN

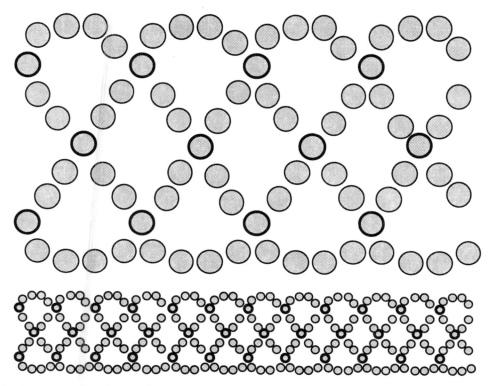

This pattern is deceptively simple in appearance but complex in execution. Start at a connector bead (see dashed line below), and make a "Figure 8" pattern of beads, connecting them through a central connector bead, and ending up at the starting bead, as shown. Now rethread (solid line) through seven beads (the last one, a connector bead, becoming the new starter bead), and create a new "Figure 8" pattern, ending up at the original connector bead, which ultimately has three threads running through it. Now rethread through the next five beads, create a new pattern, then rethread through existing beads to a new starter connector bead. Continue. Note how the rethread patterns alternate: Seven beads along the inside, or five outside. The rethreaded segments form a continuous undulating pattern throughout the piece.

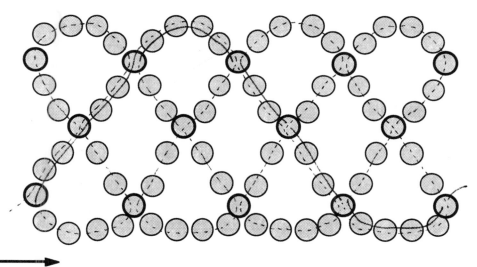

PAGODA EARRINGS

These are fairly easy to make, and with the right colors, perfect for Christmas. Use about 12 inches of beading thread for each earring. Start with the top connector bead (dark rimmed), and end by going through the top connector bead, forming a connecting ring of beads, and then meeting the beginning thread for the final knots. Use long nose pliers to connect the earrings to earring findings.

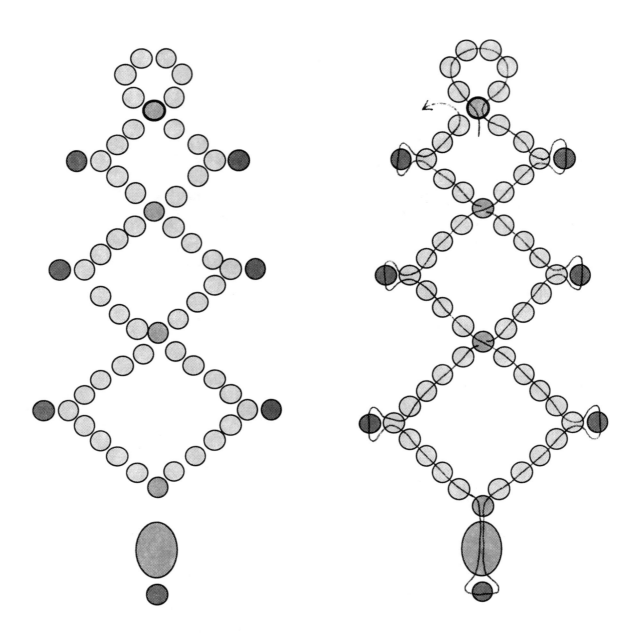

DANGLING DIAMOND EARRINGS

Here's another easy set of earrings that use very small seed beads (size 14/°) with the usual size 10/° or 11/° hex cut beads (see Materials and Types of Beads). Use about 12 inches of beading thread for each earring. Thread a needle on each end of the thread. Tension holds the diamonds in place, so start from the bottommost bead (below the large dangle bead), and work your way up both sides, drawing the threads taut to form the diamonds. Use long nose pliers to attach to earring findings. *Variation*: substitute short bugle beads for the hex cut beads to create more pronounced diamonds.

⬤ = size 14 bead   ◯ = hex cut bead

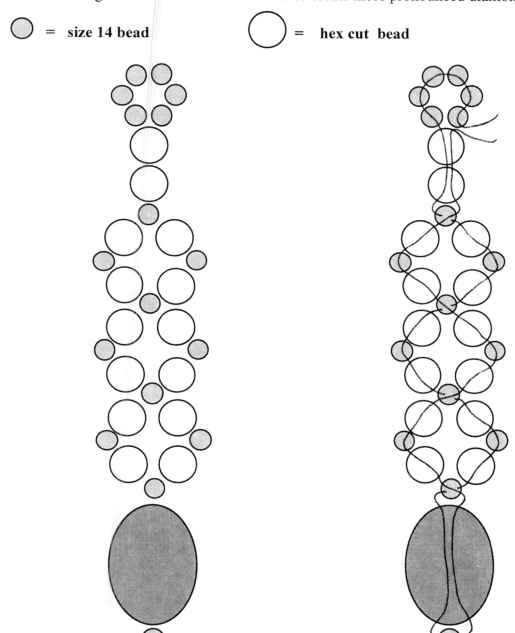

SPIDER WEB EARRINGS

Although these look complicated, they can be made relatively quickly. From an initial circle of 10 beads, you add on five groups each of three beads, five beads, seven beads, and 11 beads. Use about 18 inches of beading thread for each earring. The dashed line shows you how to wend the thread at the end back to the beginning in the middle to end the piece.

22

CHAIN LINK NECKLACE

This modified **MEDALLION** pattern can be done at least three ways, using one or two threads. To curve the necklace, there should be one less bead in the upper parts of the loops: Five beads here, as opposed to six beads in the lower part. Here, seed beads are substituted for medallion beads, and the circle size varies to create a chain link effect. See MEDALLION PATTERN (Page 15) for one way, using one thread that threads in two directions, back and forth. The same threading pattern can be done with two threads threading in one direction, shown here. A third way involves one thread that threads in one direction, also shown here. *Variation*: Put the medallions back in to create a curving medallion necklace! Vary the size of the alternating circles of beads.

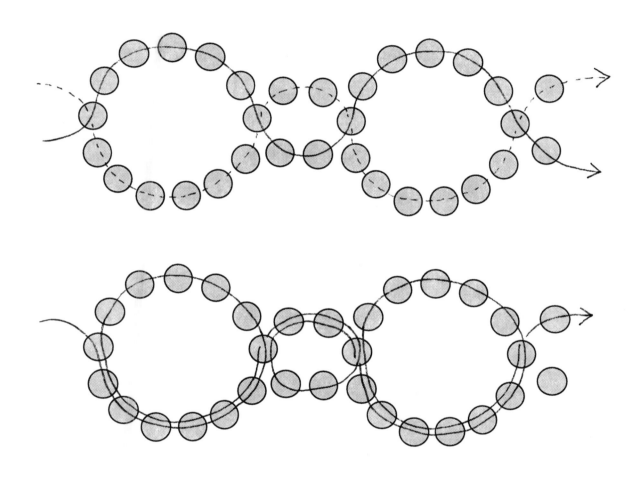

HULA HOOP NECKLACE: 2 THREAD NECKLACES

This is the first of the 2-thread necklace designs offered here: One thread forms the neckline, while a second, design thread connects the design to the first with various neckline connector beads. AS IN ALL TWO THREAD NECKLACES, string the neckline thread first, and flag with tape at either end to prevent slippage. Then work the design thread onto it. Adjust the taped ends of the neckline as the connected design introduces tension into the neckline. End the necklaces as you begin them, with the design thread going through a length of the neckline beads (referred to as lead beads) before beginning the design pattern. When larger dangling beads are needed (especially if using monofiliament), make sure the beads are at least 6mm in size (or of equivalent weight) so that they will hang properly. Smaller beads may be used with nymo thread.

For this pattern, create a neckline of 236 beads (about 13.5 inches). There are seven lead beads on either end, six neckline beads between connectors (five shown below), and 37 interconnecting circles of 15 beads each. *Variations*: vary the size of the hoops, make the bottommost bead a larger one, add a dangling larger bead or group of beads at the bottom of each hoop, increase the number of connector beads . . .

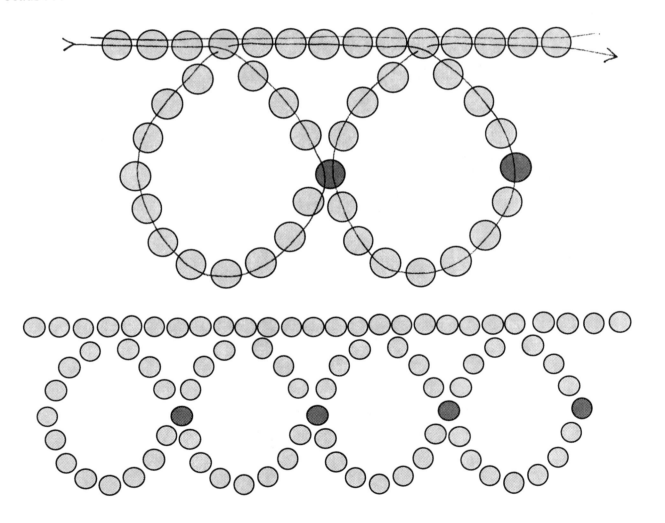

24

PENNANT CHOKER NECKLACE

Use beading thread for this two string, 12 inch choker. There are four lead beads at either end, eight beads between neckline connectors, 12 beads on the vertical strands, six beads on the bottom arches, and a total of 20 patterns with alternating dangling beads. To start the pattern, string the design thread through the first section three times (down, up, & down) as shown, then do the rest of the pattern as shown. Note the highlighted junctures. Depending on the neck size, adjust your neckline thread length and the number of patterns needed.

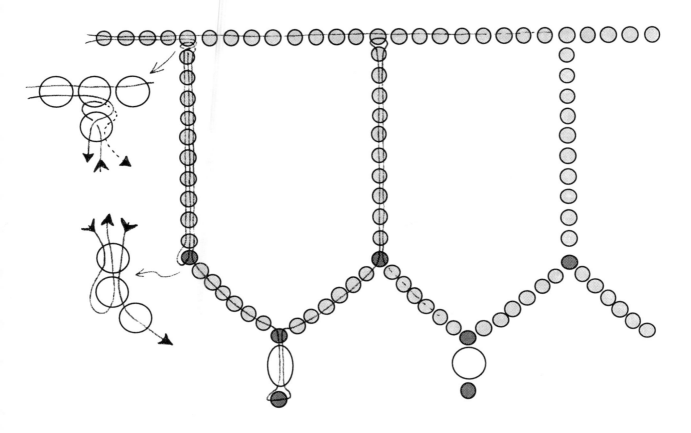

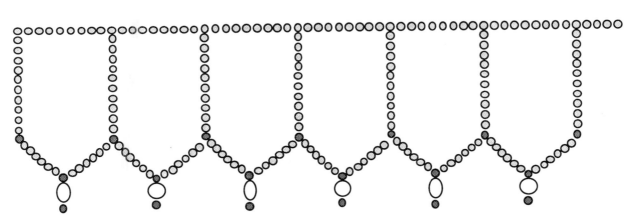

25

JULIA'S NECKLACE

My seven year old daughter (at the time), Julia, drew the initial design of this two thread, 18 inch necklace. It is a simple but elegant piece that can be made relatively quickly. Create a neckline of 314 beads. There are six lead beads at either end, six beads between each group of five neckline connector beads, five beads on each of the upper arches, eight beads on each of the lower arches, 27 larger dangle beads, and a total of 28 patterns (two triangles and a larger lower triangle with a dangle bead).

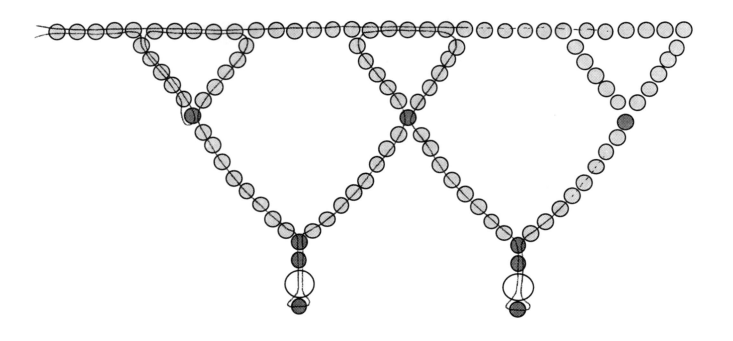

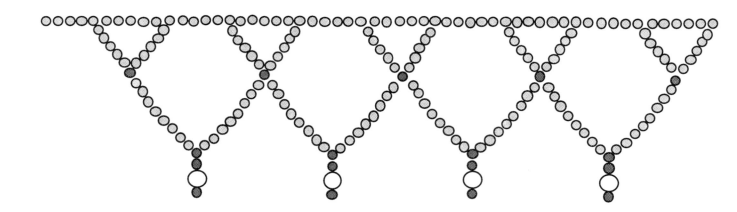

EMPRESS CHOKER NECKLACE

This two thread necklace is evocative of bygone times, and can be made relatively quickly; the design thread is a modified diamond lace pattern. Create a neckline of 191 beads (about 11.5 inches). There are no lead beads, nine beads between neckline connectors, five beads on each of the upper and middle arches, six beads on the lower arches, and 19 large hanging beads of two alternating types. Add to the pattern as needed. Knot threads at each end together and attach to a short chain, or just jump rings, and a clasp. Add on lead beads or more patterns for larger necks. Wear With Pride!

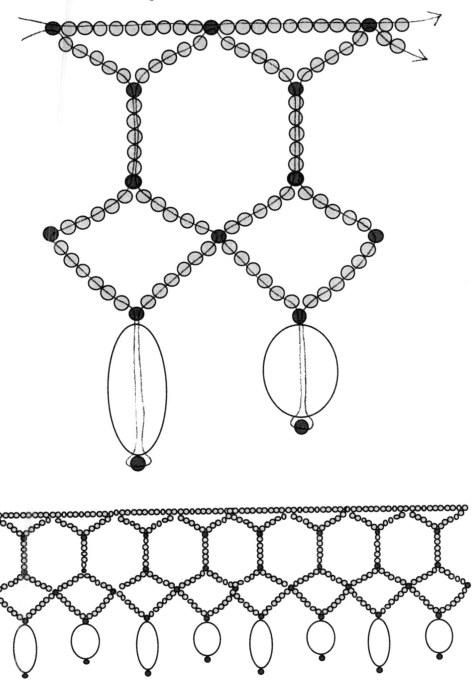

HANGING BEAD NECKLACE

Use beading thread. Create a neckline of 351 beads (about 19 inches), and hang beads of different sizes and colors from the dark connector beads. There are 10 lead beads before the first and after the last neckline connectors, nine beads between neckline connectors, five beads between connectors on each arch, eight beads from which the largest bead dangles, six beads from which the other large beads dangle, and 33 large beads. *Variations:* Vary the dangle lengths, arch lengths and neckline connectors (from singles to groups).

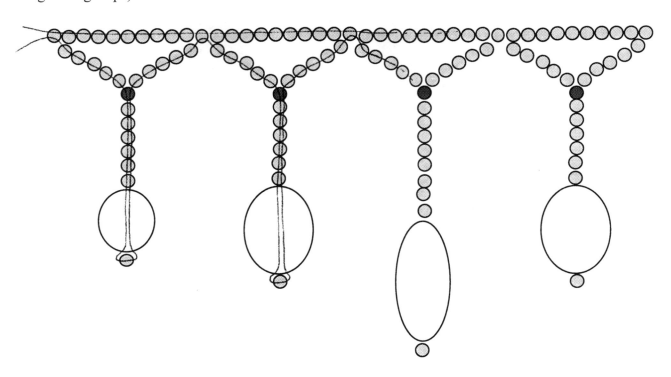

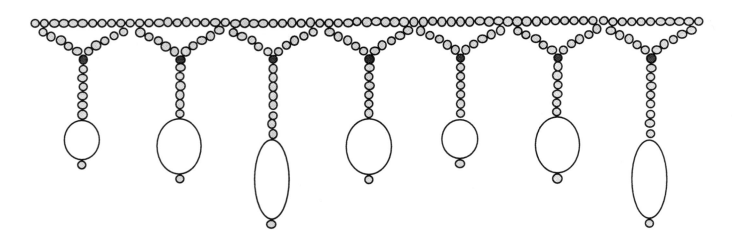

JULIA'S LOOPY NECKLACE

At eight years old, Julia presented me with another design, which is a modified hanging bead pattern. Use beading thread and create a neckline of 415 beads (about 13 inches), with seven beads before and after the first and last neckline connectors. Here, loops of 29 beads are substituted for every other large hanging bead, to create 13 loops and 12 dangling beads. There are seven beads between neckline connectors, and five beads for each arch.

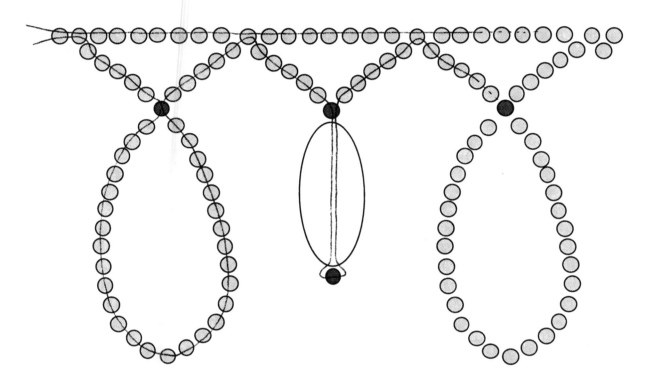

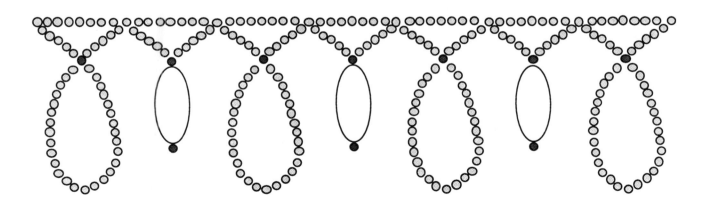

VALENTINE NECKLACE

This is a wide, curved, two thread, 17.3 inch necklace, made of 1, 446 iridescent clear red, 390 clear green and 193 gold, 11/° seed beads forming 14 red hearts interspersed with green. Other beads include: 14 milky white drop beads (bottom of heart), 14 clear red 1/4" heart beads (mid-heart), and 13 faceted honey amber 1/4" crystals (bottom of green area). String 312 red beads on the neckline thread. String the design thread through 12 of the neckline beads and begin the pattern as shown below. Note that the design thread goes through the dangle bead below the heart twice. Start and end with a heart. String the design thread through the last 12 neckline beads. Finis!

◐ = red   ● = green   ◯ = connectors: red on neck; gold on design

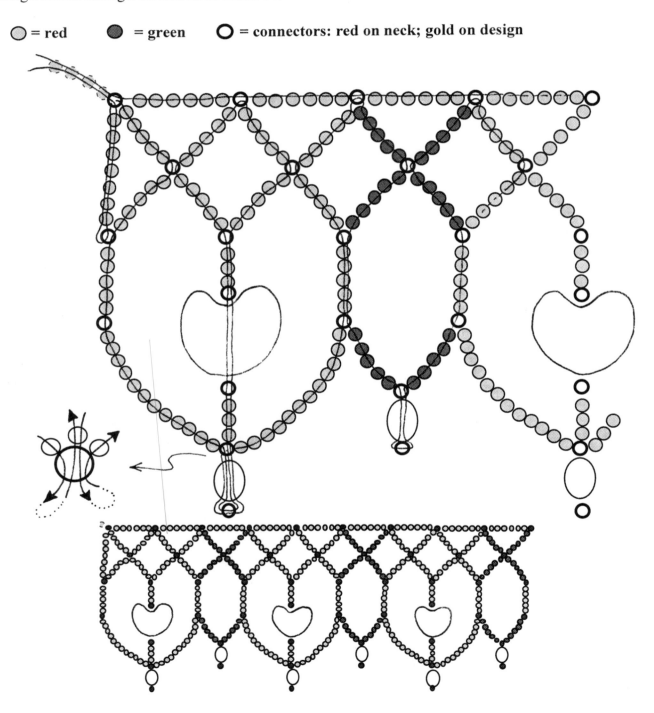

EARRING DESIGNS BY SIG
by
Sigrid Wynne-Evans

Eureka! This book provides the answer to often repeated requests for new and different beading designs and included are some of the best. Both experienced and beginning beaders will cherish this treasure trove of 46 unique designs, all made with the Brick (or Comanche) Stitch technique. The designs will also thrill applique beadworkers who can incorporate these fresh ideas into their projects. Featuring contemporary and Native American themes, the designs focus on images rather than standard geometric patterns.

This book feature complete, illustrated instructions, bead-by-bead patterns for each project and 8 pages in full color.

Designs include: Tropical Fish, Mermaid, Snake, Hummingbird, Dragonfly, Show Girl, Bird On A Swing, Toucan, Beagle, Seahorse, Desert Tapestry, Dragon, Flamingo, Beaded Bear, Navajo Rug, Desert Horse, Midnight Coyote, Spirit Dancer, Pegasus, Moon Goddess, Thunderbird, Peacock, Parrot, Rain Keeper, Polar Bear, Elephant, Egyptian, Phoenix, Frog, Iris, AND MORE!

A BEADWORK COMPANION: A Step-by-Step Illustrated Workbook for Beading Projects
by
Jean Heinbuch

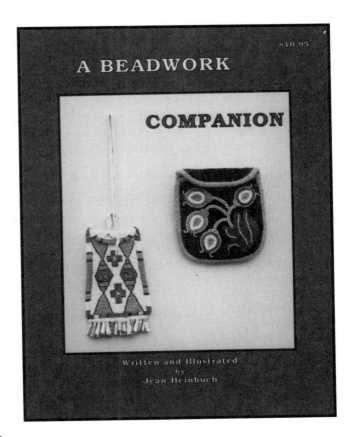

This exciting new book presents step-by step instructions for making 11 beautiful beading craft projects from barrettes to fully beaded belts. Beading patterns are provided for each project, along with 7 additional beading patterns. Photos of each item and over 200 illustrations are included!

In 112 pages, the construction and beading of the following projects are described in "How To Do It" detail: Large Barrette, Heart-Shaped Barrette, Rosette Hair Ties, Ration Ticket Bag, Strike-A-Light Bag, Round Floral Belt Buckle, Neck Knife Sheath, Large Old Style Knife Sheath, Wrap Around Knife Sheath, Geometric Pattern Beaded Belt, and Floral Beaded Belt.

The introduction discusses Materials, Construction Stitches (Return Stitch, Gourd Stitch & Lazy Stitch), Beading Techniques and Beaded Edges (Oblique, Loop, Lazy Stitch & Gourd Stitch). The book contains projects for all levels of beaders, from beginning to advanced.

SOME EAGLE'S VIEW BESTSELLERS THAT MAY BE OF INTEREST:

❑ Eagle's View Publishing Catalog of Books	B00/99	$3.00
❑ The Technique of Porcupine Quill Decoration/Orchard	B00/01	$8.95
❑ The Technique of North American Indian Beadwork/Smith	B00/02	$10.95
❑ Techniques of Beading Earrings by Deon DeLange	B00/03	$8.95
❑ More Techniques of Beading Earrings by Deon DeLange	B00/04	$8.95
❑ America's *First* First World War: The French & Indian	B00/05	$8.95
❑ Crow Indian Beadwork/Wildschut and Ewers	B00/06	$8.95
❑ New Adventures in Beading Earrings by Laura Reid	B00/07	$8.95
❑ North American Indian Burial Customs by Dr. H. C. Yarrow	B00/09	$9.95
❑ Traditional Indian Crafts by Monte Smith	B00/10	$9.95
❑ Traditional Indian Bead & Leather Crafts/ Smith/VanSickle	B00/11	$9.95
❑ Indian Clothing of the Great Lakes: 1740-1840/Hartman	B00/12	$10.95
❑ Shinin' Trails: A Possibles Bag of Fur Trade Trivia by Legg	B00/13	$7.95
❑ Adventures in Creating Earrings by Laura Reid	B00/14	$9.95
❑ Circle of Power by William Higbie	B00/15	$7.95
❑ Etienne Provost: Man of the Mountains by Jack Tykal	B00/16	$9.95
❑ A Quillwork Companion by Jean Heinbuch	B00/17	$9.95
❑ Making Indian Bows & Arrows...The Old Way/Wallentine	B00/18	$10.95
❑ Making Arrows...The Old Way by Doug Wallentine	B00/19	$4.00
❑ Hair of the Bear: Campfire Yarns & Stories by Eric Bye	B00/20	$9.95
❑ How To Tan Skins The Indian Way by Evard Gibby	B00/21	$4.50
❑ A Beadwork Companion by Jean Heinbuch	B00/22	$10.95
❑ Beads and Cabochons by Patricia Lyman	B00/23	$9.95
❑ Earring Designs by Sig: Book I by Sigrid Wynne-Evans	B00/24	$8.95
❑ Creative Crafts by Marj by Marj Schneider	B00/25	$9.95
❑ How To Bead Earrings by Lori Berry	B00/26	$10.95
❑ Delightful Beaded Earring Designs by Jan Radford	B00/27	$8.95
❑ Earring Designs by Sig: Book II by Sigrid Wynne-Evans	B00/28	$8.95
❑ Craft Cord Corral by Janice S. Ackerman	B00/30	$8.95
❑ Classic Earring Designs by Nola May	B00/32	$9.95
❑ How To Make Primitive Pottery by Evard Gibby	B00/33	$8.95
❑ Plains Indian & Mountain Man Arts and Crafts by C. Overstreet	B00/34	$13.95
❑ Beaded Images: Intricate Beaded Jewelry by Barbara Elbe	B00/35	$9.95
❑ Earring Designs by Sig-Book III: Celebrations by Sigrid Wynne-Evans	B00/36	$9.95
❑ Techniques of Fashion Earrings by Deon DeLange	B00/37	$9.95
❑ Beaded Images II: Intricate Beaded Jewelry by Barbara Elbe	B00/38	$9.95
❑ Picture Beaded Earrings for Beginners by Starr Steil	B00/39	$9.95
❑ Plains Indian & Mountain Man Arts and Crafts II by C. Overstreet	B00/40	$12.95

• •

At your local bookstore or use this handy form for ordering :

EAGLE'S VIEW PUBLISHING READERS SERVICE, DEPT SLAO
6756 North Fork Road - Liberty, Utah 84310

Please send me the above title(s). I am enclosing $_____ (Please add $2.50 per order to cover shipping and handling.) Send check or money order - no cash or C.O.D.s please.

Ms./Mrs./Mr. _____

Address _____

City/State/Zip Code _____

Prices and availability subject to change without notice. Allow 3 to 4 weeks for delivery.

SLAO - 8/96